I. Introduction

A. Introduction of the importance of passive income in generating wealth

B. Explanation of the role of artificial intelligence in creating passive income

C. Presentation of the objective of the live event: to provide 50 ideas for passive income methods using artificial intelligence

II. 10 passive income methods related to artificial intelligence in the finance industry
A. Explanation of the role of AI in finance

B. Presentation of 10 passive income methods in this field

III. 10 passive income methods related to artificial intelligence in advertising and marketing
A. Explanation of the role of AI in advertising and marketing
B. Presentation of 10 passive income methods in this field

IV. 10 passive income methods related to artificial intelligence in the health industry
A. Explanation of the role of AI in health
B. Presentation of 10 passive income methods in this field

V. 10 passive income methods related to artificial intelligence in education
A. Explanation of the role of AI in education
B. Presentation of 10 passive income methods in this field

VI. Conclusion

I. Introduction

For years, finding effective ways to generate passive income has been a major concern for many individuals seeking to create a source of wealth and financial stability. Technological advancements in recent years have made this pursuit easier and more optimized, notably through the use of artificial intelligence (AI).

In this book, we offer a thorough exploration of 50 different methods for generating passive income using AI, covering various sectors such as finance, advertising and marketing, health, and education. We have carefully selected these methods to provide a comprehensive overview of the possibilities for using AI to generate passive income in different sectors.

In the first part of this book, we will examine the role of AI in the finance sector, presenting 10 methods of passive income that can be used in this field. In the second part, we will focus on the advertising and marketing domain, exploring 10 methods of passive income using AI. The third part will look at the opportunities offered by AI in the health sector, presenting 10 methods of passive income. Finally, we will examine the role of AI in education, presenting 10 methods of passive income using AI in this field.

Our goal is to provide you with the knowledge and inspiration needed to explore the exciting world of passive income based on AI. Whether you are looking to supplement your income or create a full-time passive income, this book will guide you through the most innovative and effective ideas for creating passive income streams using AI. You will discover how this technology can significantly improve your financial situation and how to leverage it to create opportunities for your financial future.

A. Introduction of the importance of passive income in generating wealth

Passive income has become a crucial element in wealth generation. Unlike active income, which is based on time and skills, passive income is income streams generated autonomously, without the need for active and constant involvement. This allows individuals to earn money without exchanging their time for money.

The advantage of passive income is that it can be accumulated over time to create a stable and sustainable source of wealth. Passive income can come from investments, real estate, copyrights, patents, online advertising, stock dividends, and much more.

It is important to note that generating passive income is not a one-day task. This requires an initial investment of time, money, and resources to build a sustainable and reliable source of income. However, once these sources of passive income are established, they can provide long-term financial stability. Furthermore, passive income also allows individuals to focus on other aspects of their lives, such as their family, passions, and personal projects, while benefiting from a regular income stream. This can offer greater flexibility and a balance between work and personal life.

B.Explanation of the role of artificial intelligence in creating passive income.

AI has become a crucial element in generating passive income. Thanks to recent technological advances, it can be used to automate and optimize various business activities, thereby enabling individuals to generate income autonomously and passively.

One key area where AI is used to generate passive income is in finance. AI algorithms can be used to analyze financial markets, predict trends, and make effective investment decisions, which can lead to higher returns for investors. Additionally, automated trading platforms using AI can generate passive income by buying and selling financial assets according to predefined parameters.

In the advertising and marketing field, AI can be used to effectively target consumers by analyzing data and identifying individual preferences. This can lead to more effective advertising campaigns and a higher return on investment for advertisers. Furthermore, AI-powered chatbots can be used to autonomously respond to customer inquiries, offering 24/7 customer service.

AI is also increasingly used in the healthcare field for generating passive income. Telemedicine applications, for example, can allow doctors to see more patients without needing to be physically present, which can generate additional passive income. Additionally, health data can be analyzed using AI to predict health trends and provide personalized treatment recommendations, which can improve patient outcomes and increase healthcare providers' revenue.

Finally, in the education field, AI can be used to automate and personalize online learning, which can lead to a more effective and cost-efficient learning experience. AI-enabled online learning platforms can generate passive income by offering automated online courses on a large scale.

B.Presentation of the objective of the book: to provide 50 ideas for generating passive income through the use of artificial intelligence.

The objective of this book is to present 50 ideas for passive income methods that can be generated through the use of artificial intelligence. AI is a technology that can make many processes more efficient and automated, which can lead to passive income opportunities in various fields.
Throughout this presentation, we will explore different ways in which AI can be used to generate passive income without having to devote significant time and effort. The ideas we will cover include concrete examples of products and services that can be used to make money without having to be constantly active.
We will also examine the advantages and disadvantages of each passive income method, as well as the considerations to take into account when implementing these ideas. Finally, we will provide you with tips and tricks to help you maximize your potential for passive income through AI.

A. Explanation of the role of AI in finance

Artificial intelligence (AI) has revolutionized the finance industry by allowing for quick and accurate analysis of financial data. But its impact is not limited to that alone. It also offers many opportunities to generate passive income in the financial sector.

Indeed, thanks to AI, financial institutions can now detect and prevent fraud more effectively, which significantly reduces losses related to fraudulent activities. This reduction in losses then translates into an increase in passive income.

Likewise, in terms of credit risk evaluation, AI algorithms can more accurately analyze borrowers' solvency, allowing financial institutions to select borrowers with better repayment guarantees and thus minimize losses.

This optimization of borrower selection also results in passive income. Regarding portfolio management, AI allows for the optimization of investments based on criteria such as risk level, investment objectives, and market conditions. By analyzing financial data and identifying trends, patterns, and correlations that are not visible to the naked eye, AI can maximize returns and minimize risks. This optimization of investment portfolios can then translate into passive income for investors.

Finally, in terms of investment analysis, AI allows for more informed decision-making by providing information on investments that are likely to perform well and those that are likely to underperform. This more informed decision-making also results in passive income.

In summary, AI offers a unique opportunity for investors to generate passive income by using innovative technologies to optimize their investments. By helping financial institutions make more informed decisions, reduce losses, and maximize returns, AI opens unprecedented prospects for the creation of passive income in the finance industry.

B. The 10 methods of passive income related to artificial intelligence in the field of finance.

Investing in the stock market assisted by AI

Investing in the stock market can be intimidating for both beginner and experienced investors. Fortunately, artificial intelligence is here to offer us valuable assistance. AI can help us analyze stock market data more effectively, allowing us to make more informed investment decisions.

With AI algorithms, we can discover trends, patterns, and correlations in stock market data that may be overlooked by human observation. This enables us to better understand market movements and predict future trends, which can increase our confidence in our investment choices.

Furthermore, AI can help us manage our investment portfolio more effectively. It can use sophisticated models to evaluate the level of risk in our investments and help us find an optimal balance between risk and return. This allows us to adjust our portfolio based on our investment goals and risk profile

The process of generating passive income by investing in the stock market assisted by AI can vary depending on the chosen investment strategy.
In general, here are the key steps to invest in the AI-assisted stock market:

The first step is to find an online brokerage platform that offers AI tools for stock investment. Some popular platforms are E-Trade, Robinhood, or Charles Schwab.
You need to create an online brokerage account and deposit funds to invest.

Next, you can use the AI tools available on the platform to analyze stock data and identify investment opportunities.

 These AI tools are capable of analyzing enormous amounts of data in a very short time, allowing you to have a more precise analysis of stocks that might interest you.

The third step is to create a balanced investment portfolio using AI models to evaluate the risk level. AI helps you determine the level of risk associated with each investment. It is important to create a well-diversified portfolio to minimize risks.

Then, you need to regularly monitor the performance of your portfolio and adjust it based on new data and market changes.

Regular monitoring of your portfolio allows you to make more informed decisions and maximize your profits.

As for useful websites for investing in the AI-assisted stock market, here are some examples:

Seeking Alpha: an investment platform that provides AI-based investment analysis and recommendations.

AlphaSense: a financial search engine that uses AI to analyze financial and stock data.

Stock Rover: an AI-based portfolio analysis platform that allows you to track the performance of your stock investments.

Betterment: a portfolio management platform that uses AI to optimize your portfolio based on your investment goals and risk profile.

Revolutionizing Trading with AI-Based Automated Trading Robots

utomated trading based on AI is a revolutionary innovation in the world of investment. AI-based trading robots are capable of analyzing real-time financial data and executing trades autonomously. This technology enables investors to benefit from speed and accuracy that humans simply cannot match.

Among the popular trading robots in the world of AI, we can find:

- **Forex Megadroid**: This robot uses sophisticated algorithms to analyze market data and execute trades autonomously. Additionally, it is known for its high success rate, making it a popular choice among investors.

- **Tradestation**: This robot also uses AI-based algorithms to execute trades and monitor the market in real-time. Additionally, it has a user-friendly interface that allows investors to customize their trading settings based on their preferences.

- **Fintech**: This robot uses machine learning algorithms to analyze market data and predict future trends. This robot is capable of identifying profitable trading opportunities and making trading decisions accordingly.

- **Haasbot**: This robot is capable of trading on multiple markets simultaneously and uses a variety of technical indicators to analyze market data and execute trades in real-time.

- **Gunbot:** This robot uses technical indicators and signals to analyze market data and execute trades autonomously. It can also take into account financial news and important economic events.

- **Qtrade:** This robot uses machine learning algorithms to analyze market data and predict future trends. It can also be programmed to execute specific trades based on certain criteria.

- **Cryptohopper:** This robot uses AI algorithms to analyze cryptocurrency market data and execute trades autonomously. It is also capable of monitoring social media trends and other sources of information to make trading decisions.

- **Axiom AI:** This robot uses machine learning algorithms to analyze market data and predict future trends. It can also be programmed to monitor economic events and financial news.

- **AlgoTrader:** This robot uses AI-based algorithms to analyze market data and execute trades autonomously. It is also capable of managing multiple trading portfolios at once.

- **DeepTrade:** This robot uses deep learning algorithms to analyze market data and predict future trends. It is also capable of managing risks and limiting potential losses.

Boost your savings with AI: Discover automatic high-yield investment applications.

assisted savings applications allow for the creation of automatic savings plans that withdraw a fixed amount from your bank account and invest it in high-yield investments. The investment apps listed above are financial tools that allow users to automatically and seamlessly invest their money in high-yield investments. These apps withdraw a fixed amount from the user's bank account at regular intervals (monthly, weekly, etc.) and invest the money in diversified portfolios. AI algorithms are used to analyze the user's spending habits and financial goals in order to customize the investment portfolio.

- . **Stash**: This software offers a variety of investment portfolios for users based on their risk tolerance and financial goals. It also offers automated savings features, such as automatic transfers from a checking account to a savings or investment account.

- **Qapital**: This software allows users to set up custom savings rules, such as savings based on their spending or purchasing habits. It also uses AI to suggest additional savings based on past spending and spending trends.

- **Digit**: This software analyzes users' spending habits to determine the optimal amount to save each month. It automatically transfers this money to a high-yield savings account.

- **Chime**: This software offers a fee-free checking account, which allows users to set up automated savings and invest in diversified portfolios. It also uses AI to analyze spending and suggest additional savings.

- **Personal Capital**: This software offers automated financial planning tools such as retirement projections and scenario simulations. It also uses AI to build personalized investment portfolios and monitor investments in real-time.

- **Robinhood**: This software offers fee-free stock trading and allows users to invest in ETFs (exchange-traded funds) and cryptocurrencies. It also uses AI to monitor markets and provide investment insights.

- **WiseBanyan** - This investment application uses AI to offer personalized investment portfolios, as well as provide investment advice.

- **Ally Invest** - This trading and investment application uses AI to monitor markets in real-time and provide personalized investment recommendations.

By using these applications, users can automatically save and invest their money in high-yield investments without actively managing their portfolio. The AI algorithms used by these applications help design personalized investment portfolios for each user, which can help maximize returns and minimize risks.

Maximize Your Passive Income with AI-based Financial Advisory Chatbots"

Personalized Financial Advice: AI-based financial advisory chatbots are capable of providing personalized financial advice based on your investor profile and financial goals.

AI-based financial advisory chatbots are computer programs that use artificial intelligence to offer personalized financial advice to users. These chatbots are designed to understand the most common financial questions and provide quick and accurate responses. They can also provide financial recommendations based on each user's preferences and financial goals.

Financial advisory chatbots are useful for people who need financial advice but do not wish to or cannot consult a financial advisor in person. They are also useful for people who are looking for quick answers to common financial questions, such as debt management, retirement planning, investment, and insurance. Financial advisory chatbots use machine learning algorithms to improve over time. The more they interact with users, the more they learn and the more accurate and useful they can be in answering financial questions.

Ultimately, AI-based financial advisory chatbots offer a convenient and efficient way to obtain personalized financial advice. They are useful for people who are looking for quick and accurate answers to common financial questions, as well as for people who cannot or do not want to consult a financial advisor in person. Here is a list of popular chatbots related to trading:

TradeHero: a virtual trading app that uses chatbots to provide information on market trends and trading tips.

TradingView: an online trading platform that uses chatbots to assist traders in monitoring the markets in real-time and making informed decisions.

Capital.com: a trading app that uses chatbots to provide market analysis and information on trading trends.

Robinhood: a trading app that uses chatbots to help users invest in stocks, mutual funds, and cryptocurrencies.

eToro: a trading platform that uses chatbots to provide information on markets, data analysis, and trading strategies.

StockTwits: an online trading community that uses chatbots to provide information on market trends, economic events, and industry news.

Zignaly: a cryptocurrency trading platform that uses chatbots to provide trading signals and information on market trends..

Automated credit analysis: AI algorithms are capable of analyzing credit data to assess borrower risk and determine appropriate interest rates.

Credit analysis is a crucial step in the borrowing process, as it allows lenders to determine the level of risk associated with a borrower and decide on the appropriate interest rate. Thanks to advances in artificial intelligence, it is now possible to automate this credit analysis.

AI algorithms use credit data to evaluate a borrower's risk based on several factors such as debt amount, payment history, credit score, and other relevant financial information. The algorithms are capable of analyzing this data exhaustively, quickly, and accurately to provide a reliable and objective evaluation of a borrower's risk.

Once the analysis is done, lenders can use the results to determine appropriate interest rates for borrowers. Low-risk borrowers are offered lower interest rates, while high-risk borrowers may be subject to higher interest rates to compensate for the increased risk level.

Automated credit analysis allows lenders to perform faster, more objective, and more accurate credit analysis than traditional methods.

This can be particularly useful for financial institutions that process a large number of credit applications each day, as it allows them to save time and reduce costs associated with hiring additional staff to perform credit analyses manually.

Ultimately, AI-based automated credit analysis provides an effective and reliable way to evaluate borrowers' risk and determine appropriate interest rates. It can help lenders make more informed decisions and offer loans that better suit borrowers' needs while reducing costs and speeding up the lending process.

AI-based Insurance: Insurance companies use AI algorithms to evaluate accident risks and offer personalized insurance premiums.

The use of AI in the insurance industry has revolutionized the way insurance companies evaluate risks and offer personalized insurance premiums.

Insurance companies use AI algorithms to analyze large amounts of data related to accidents, claims, driving profiles, etc., to determine the level of risk associated with each client. The results of this analysis are used to propose personalized insurance premiums that correspond to the individual risk level of each client.

There are several software programs that use AI for risk analysis and insurance pricing. For example, Lemonade is an insurance company that uses AI to evaluate claims and determine whether they are valid or not.

AI is also used to determine the level of risk associated with each client and offer personalized insurance premiums.

Another example is the American company Metromile, which uses AI to track the miles driven by drivers and offer insurance premiums accordingly. Drivers who travel fewer miles pay less than those who travel more miles.

Finally, Root is another insurance company that uses AI to evaluate the risk associated with each driver and offer personalized insurance premiums.

Root uses a mobile application to track each client's driving and collect data on their speed, braking, turning, etc. This data is analyzed by AI to determine the level of risk associated with each driver.

These examples demonstrate how AI is used to generate passive income in the insurance sector by offering personalized insurance premiums.

Insurance companies that use these software programs can reduce their operational costs by automating the risk assessment process and offering more accurate and personalized insurance premiums. This can also lead to better customer satisfaction, as customers feel better understood and only pay for the level of risk associated with their individual profile

Automated Bank Account Management: AI-assisted budget management applications can track expenses and suggest personalized saving and investment strategies

The use of AI in automated bank account management is an effective solution for entrepreneurs looking to generate passive income.

 AI-assisted budget management applications are capable of tracking expenses, analyzing spending habits, and offering personalized savings and investment strategies.

Examples of these applications include Mint, Personal Capital, and YNAB (You Need A Budget). Mint is a popular application that allows users to track expenses, create personalized budgets, monitor bank accounts and credit cards, and receive personalized financial advice.

Personal Capital is another wealth management application that allows users to track expenses and investments, monitor assets and debts, and provide personalized financial advice.

YNAB (You Need A Budget) is a budget management application that helps users plan their budget, track their expenses, save money, and pay off their debts.

The application uses a four-rule budgeting method that allows users to control their expenses and achieve their long-term financial goals.

By using these AI-assisted budget management applications, entrepreneurs can have better visibility into their finances and improve their cash management, which can lead to more efficient use of their resources and business growth.

Additionally, by using these applications, entrepreneurs can reduce financial management costs by automating certain tasks and avoiding human errors.

 In conclusion, the use of AI in automated bank account management can be an effective method for entrepreneurs to generate passive income, improve their financial management, and reduce costs.

 AI-assisted budget management applications such as Mint, Personal Capital, and YNAB can help entrepreneurs track their expenses, save money, and achieve their long-term financial goals.

Economic Forecasting: AI models can predict economic trends and market fluctuations, enabling informed investment decisions.

AI models offer an interesting solution for entrepreneurs who are looking to make more informed investment decisions by predicting economic trends and market fluctuations.

These AI models are capable of processing a large amount of economic and financial data and analyzing it to predict future trends.

Software such as QuantConnect, AlphaSense, and Kensho are used by investors and portfolio managers to benefit from these accurate and fast economic forecasts.

QuantConnect is an open-source platform that allows investors to develop and test AI-based automated investment strategies.

The platform offers historical data, visualization tools, and backtesting to enable users to test their algorithms before deploying them on real-time markets.

AlphaSense is an AI-powered enterprise search engine that allows users to find relevant financial and economic information for their business.

The platform analyzes data from millions of financial documents to provide accurate information and forecasts on financial markets and economic trends.

Kensho is a financial data analysis platform that uses AI to analyze market data and predict future fluctuations.

The platform is used by portfolio managers to identify investment opportunities, potential risks, and market trends.

By using these AI-assisted economic forecasting software, entrepreneurs can make more informed investment decisions and potentially generate long-term passive income.

The ability to predict economic trends and market fluctuations allows entrepreneurs to make informed decisions to invest in profitable opportunities and avoid unnecessary financial risks.

Automated Risk Management: Banks and insurance companies use AI algorithms to evaluate risks and propose coverage strategies

Automated risk management is an effective method for banks and insurance companies to assess risks and propose coverage strategies.

AI algorithms are used to process historical data, market trends, and customer information to identify potential risks and propose appropriate coverage strategies

In addition to the previously mentioned software, other platforms like RiskAI and RiskSense are used by financial institutions to manage risks effectively.

RiskAI is an AI platform that allows businesses to manage risks and make evidence-based decisions. The platform uses machine learning algorithms to analyze data and identify potential risks.

RiskSense is an AI platform that helps companies assess risks and manage vulnerabilities.

The platform uses advanced analytics and machine learning algorithms to identify risks and provide prioritized remediation options.

By using these AI software solutions to manage risks, banks and insurance companies can make more informed decisions to cover potential risks and avoid financial losses. Moreover, the use of these software solutions can offer opportunities for generating long-term passive income by effectively managing risks and improving the financial performance of the company.

RiskSense is an AI platform that helps companies assess risks and manage vulnerabilities.

The platform uses advanced analytics and machine learning algorithms to identify risks and provide prioritized remediation options.

By using these AI software solutions to manage risks, banks and insurance companies can make more informed decisions to cover potential risks and avoid financial losses. Moreover, the use of these software solutions can offer opportunities for generating long-term passive income by effectively managing risks and improving the financial performance of the company.

Automated Portfolio Analysis

Automated Portfolio Analysis: AI-assisted portfolio analysis applications allow you to track the performance of your investments and suggest adjustments to maximize returns .

Automated portfolio analysis: AI-assisted portfolio analysis applications allow you to track the performance of your investments and propose adjustments to maximize returns.

AI-assisted portfolio analysis applications are an effective solution for new investors looking to generate passive income. These applications use AI algorithms to track investment performance and propose adjustments to maximize returns.

Software such as Personal Capital, Betterment, and Wealthfront are examples of AI-assisted portfolio analysis applications. Personal Capital is an online tool that allows users to track their investment portfolio performance, monitor their expenses, and plan for retirement.

The platform uses AI algorithms to analyze market and portfolio data and provide recommendations to maximize returns.

Betterment is an online investment platform that uses AI algorithms to create customized portfolios for investors.
The platform uses historical market data and user investment preferences to create a diversified portfolio that matches their return and risk goals.

Wealthfront is another online investment platform that uses AI algorithms to create customized portfolios for investors.
The platform uses historical market data and user investment preferences to create a diversified portfolio that matches their return and risk goals.

By using these AI-assisted portfolio analysis applications, new investors can generate long-term passive income by effectively tracking their investments and maximizing their returns.

These software options also provide a convenient option for investors who don't have the time or expertise to manage their investment portfolio independently.

III.The 10 Methods of Passive Income Related to Artificial Intelligence in Advertising and Marketing

A. Explanation of the Role of AI in Advertising and Marketing

Artificial Intelligence (AI) has revolutionized many industries, and advertising and marketing are no exception. Indeed, AI plays a key role in these fields by enabling a better understanding of consumers and offering them targeted and personalized ads.

First, it is important to define what AI is in the context of advertising and marketing. AI can be defined as the use of computer techniques to analyze data and perform tasks that would normally require human intelligence, such as pattern recognition or decision-making. In the field of advertising and marketing, AI is used to collect and analyze data on consumers in order to better understand their behaviors and preferences.

One of the main advantages of using AI in advertising and marketing is the ability to collect and analyze large amounts of data in real-time. Companies can thus obtain valuable information about consumer behaviors, interests, preferences, and even moods. This data is then used to create targeted and personalized ads that are more likely to catch consumers' attention and encourage them to purchase.

AI is also used to automate some tasks in the ad creation process. For example, it can be used to create real-time personalized ads based on data collected on consumers. It can also be used to optimize ad campaigns by adjusting bids on ads based on previous campaign results.

Another important role of AI in advertising and marketing is the ability to predict consumer behavior. By analyzing consumers' browsing, search, and transaction data, AI can predict their buying intentions, allowing them to offer relevant ads at the right time and place.

Finally, AI is also used to improve the customer experience. By using AI-powered chatbots, companies can provide quick and personalized responses to customer inquiries. Chatbots can also help customers find products or services that meet their specific needs.

In conclusion, AI has revolutionized the field of advertising and marketing by enabling companies to better understand consumers, create targeted and personalized ads, and optimize ad campaigns. It is also used to improve the customer experience by providing quick and personalized responses to customer inquiries. Companies that use AI in their advertising and marketing activities are therefore better positioned to succeed in a constantly evolving competitive environment.

B. Presentation of 10 Methods of Passive Income in Advertising and Marketing

Affiliate Marketing Boosted by AI

Affiliate marketing is becoming an increasingly popular method for generating passive income in the world of marketing and advertising. With the help of artificial intelligence (AI), companies are now able to identify potential affiliates and create personalized marketing strategies to promote their products or services more effectively. In order to facilitate this process, several companies are now offering affiliate marketing software equipped with powerful AI tools.

One of the leading companies in this field is ShareASale. Their affiliate marketing platform utilizes advanced tracking and analytics tools to help companies identify the top-performing affiliates and enable them to create customized marketing campaigns to promote their products. This can include everything from social media marketing to email campaigns and even content marketing.

Commission Junction, also known as CJ Affiliate, is another major player in the affiliate marketing industry. Their affiliate marketing platform uses AI algorithms to optimize the distribution of marketing campaigns across various channels and help companies reach a wider audience. They also offer advanced analytics tools that allow companies to track the performance of their campaigns and make adjustments as needed.

Other companies offering AI-powered tools for affiliate marketing include Impact, Partnerize, Rakuten Advertising, and Awin. These companies offer a range of advanced features such as audience segmentation, content personalization, and conversion optimization to help companies maximize their passive income through affiliate marketing.

One of the biggest advantages of using AI-powered tools for affiliate marketing is the ability to optimize campaigns for specific audiences. By analyzing data on customer behavior and preferences, AI algorithms can identify the most effective marketing strategies for reaching different segments of the market. This can help companies increase conversions and generate more passive income with less effort.

Another advantage of using AI in affiliate marketing is the ability to automate certain tasks, such as tracking and analyzing data. This can free up valuable time and resources for companies, allowing them to focus on other revenue-generating activities. AI-powered chatbots can also be used to provide customer support around the clock, reducing the need for human customer service representatives and further increasing efficiency.

As AI continues to evolve and become more sophisticated, the potential applications for affiliate marketing will only continue to grow. From personalized recommendations to dynamic pricing and more, AI-powered tools are revolutionizing the way companies approach affiliate marketing and generating passive income.

Programmatic Advertising: The Key to Effectively Targeting Your Audience and Maximizing Your Profits.

Programmatic Advertising: An Automated Process That Utilizes AI Algorithms to Buy and Sell Ad Spaces Programmatic advertising is an automated process that uses AI algorithms to buy and sell ad spaces. Advertisers have the ability to target specific audiences by using data such as browsing behaviors, interests, and purchasing preferences.

By using AI, buyers can purchase ad spaces more efficiently, ensuring that their ads reach their target audience at the right time and in the right place. Publishers, on the other hand, can maximize their revenue by selling their ad spaces at the best possible price while ensuring that their content is aligned with the needs of their advertiser clients.

Programmatic advertising also allows for greater transparency and better management of the advertising supply chain by reducing intermediaries and increasing the efficiency of buying and selling ad spaces. Ultimately, this can lead to more effective advertising campaigns for advertisers as well as higher advertising revenues for publishers.

Here are 10 applications of AI in the field of programmatic advertising:

- **SmartyAds:** This programmatic advertising platform uses AI algorithms to help advertisers target the most relevant audiences in real-time. Publishers can also optimize their revenue by selling ad spaces through auctions.

- **Google AdWords:** Google uses AI to improve the relevance and quality of ads displayed through its programmatic advertising platform. Advertisers can target audiences based on their search and browsing behavior.

- **Facebook Ads:** Facebook's programmatic advertising uses AI to target users based on their interests, browsing habits, and behavior on the social network. Advertisers can also use AI algorithms to optimize ad content based on each user's preferences.

- **AppNexus:** This programmatic advertising platform uses AI to predict the performance of ad campaigns and optimize bids to maximize publisher revenue.

- **Adroll:** Adroll uses AI to target audiences based on their browsing behavior, online purchases, and social media interactions. Advertisers can also use AI to optimize ad content and bids in real-time.

- **Simpli.fi:** This programmatic advertising platform uses AI to target local audiences and location-based audiences. Advertisers can also use AI to optimize bids based on inventory quality.

- **The Trade Desk:** This programmatic advertising platform uses AI to optimize bids in real-time and maximize ad campaign performance. Advertisers can also use AI to target audiences based on their online behavior and social interactions.

- **MediaMath:** This programmatic advertising platform uses AI to optimize bids and maximize publisher revenue. Advertisers can also use AI to target audiences based on their interests, online behavior, and social behavior.

- **TubeMogul:** This programmatic advertising platform uses AI to target audiences based on their online video watching behavior. Advertisers can also use AI to optimize bids in real-time and improve video ad campaign performance.

- **OpenX:** This programmatic advertising platform uses AI to optimize bids and maximize publisher revenue. Advertisers can also use AI to target audiences based on their online behavior and social interactions.

Prediction of future behaviors using machine learning

Predictive analysis is a technique that uses machine learning algorithms to analyze data and identify trends or patterns that can help predict future behavior. In the context of advertising and marketing, predictive analysis can help companies anticipate which campaigns and offers will be most effective in generating revenue.

Companies can use predictive models to analyze customer data such as buying habits, browsing behavior, and purchase preferences. Using this data, algorithms can predict future customer behavior and help companies develop more effective advertising and marketing strategies.

 For example, using predictive analysis, a retail company can predict which products will be most popular during the upcoming season and adjust their advertising campaigns accordingly. Similarly, a financial services company can use predictive analysis to predict the most popular financial products among its customers and develop targeted advertising campaigns to promote these products.

Ultimately, predictive analysis can help companies maximize their return on advertising investment by allowing them to target the most effective campaigns to reach their target audience. By using machine learning to identify trends and patterns in data, predictive analysis can help companies anticipate future customer behavior and develop more targeted and effective advertising strategies.

There are many predictive analytics software available, each with its own features and tasks. Here is a brief description of some of them:

- **IBM SPSS:** This data analysis software is used for statistical and regression analysis. It can also be used for predictive analysis, using machine learning algorithms to identify trends and make predictions.

- **RapidMiner:** This software allows users to create predictive analysis models using a drag-and-drop interface. It also offers data analysis, data mining, and data visualization features. Microsoft Azure Machine Learning: This cloud service allows users to create predictive analysis models using visual tools and machine learning algorithms. It can be integrated with other Microsoft cloud services, such as Power BI.

- **SAS:** This data analysis software offers a wide range of features, including predictive analysis. It uses statistical and machine learning techniques to identify trends and patterns in data.

- **Google Cloud Machine Learning:** This cloud service allows users to create predictive analysis models using visual tools and machine learning algorithms. It can be integrated with other Google cloud services, such as BigQuery and Cloud Storage.

- **KNIME:** This open-source software offers data mining, data analysis, and predictive analysis features. It can be used to create machine learning models using a drag-and-drop interface.

- **Alteryx:** This software allows users to prepare, clean, and analyze data using visual tools. It also offers predictive analysis features using machine learning algorithms.

- **H2O.ai:** This open-source software is designed for large-scale data analysis and predictive analysis. It uses machine learning algorithms to make predictions and identify trends in data.

- **DataRobot:** This software uses machine learning algorithms to create predictive analysis models using a drag-and-drop interface. It also offers model validation and process automation features.

- **Databricks:** This cloud service allows users to create predictive analysis models using visual tools and machine learning algorithms. It can be integrated with other Databricks cloud services, such as Delta Lake and MLflow.

To generate passive income from predictive analysis, a company can use the forecasts generated by the models to make informed business decisions. For example, a retail company can use demand forecasts generated by a predictive analysis model to make decisions about inventory management and pricing.

Generate passive income using AI-powered recommendation engines.

AI-powered recommendation engines are increasingly popular applications in the field of online sales. They work by collecting and analyzing data on a user's purchasing preferences, such as past purchases, viewed products, feedback left, etc.

This data is then used to generate personalized recommendations for that user. For example, if a user has purchased kitchen-related products, the recommendation engine may suggest similar products such as cooking utensils or recipe books.

Recommendation engines can use a variety of machine learning methods to analyze the data and generate recommendations. Among the most common methods are collaborative filtering algorithms and neural networks.

Collaborative filtering is a method that identifies similarities between the preferences of different users and recommends products based on those similarities. Neural networks are a more advanced method that uses complex mathematical models to identify correlations and trends in user data.

These methods are particularly effective in generating accurate and personalized recommendations for users, which can increase the likelihood of a sale. By using recommendation engines, businesses can generate passive revenue by increasing the average order value and encouraging repeat purchases from customers.

There are several methods of personalized recommendations that businesses can use to increase their passive revenue through predictive analysis. Here are some of the most common methods:

- **Collaborative filtering:** This method uses users' past preferences and behaviors to recommend products or services similar to those they have already purchased or viewed.

- Collaborative filtering systems can be based on models using clustering or classification techniques to identify groups of users with similar preferences.

- **Content-based recommendations:** This method uses the characteristics of the products or services themselves to recommend similar products or services.

Content-based recommendation systems can be based on the analysis of text, images, or other specific product features.

- **Deep learning:** This method uses neural networks to identify patterns in user data and make recommendations based on those patterns.

- Deep learning-based recommendation systems can detect complex relationships between user data and recommended products or services.

- **Bandit exploration:** This method uses an exploration-exploitation approach to recommend products or services to users. Bandit exploration-based recommendation systems can optimize recommendations based on user preferences, exploiting the user's prior knowledge while exploring new options to maximize sales chances.

- **Language models:** This method uses language models to predict users' next actions. Language models can be used to recommend products or services based on the probability that the user will perform a specific action.

- **Hybrid recommendation systems:** This method combines several recommendation methods to obtain more accurate and personalized results.

For example, a hybrid recommendation system can combine collaborative filtering techniques with content-based recommendation techniques to recommend products or services that are similar to those the user has already purchased or viewed, but also have specific features that match the user's preferences.

By using one of these methods or a combination of several of them, businesses can generate personalized recommendations for users, thereby increasing the probability of a sale and generating passive revenue.

Sentiment analysis is a powerful technique that can help businesses understand customer opinions about their brand or products.

By using AI-powered sentiment analysis algorithms, businesses can extract valuable insights from sources such as social media, online forums, and customer feedback.

By analyzing customer sentiments, businesses can discover the aspects of their brand or products that customers like or dislike, as well as the underlying reasons for these opinions.

This can help businesses identify areas that need improvement, as well as areas that are particularly appreciated by customers.

By using this information to adjust their marketing and product development strategies, businesses can improve customer satisfaction and strengthen their brand reputation. This can in turn lead to increased sales, as well as customer retention. In summary,

AI-powered sentiment analysis is a valuable tool for businesses looking to improve their market positioning and generate passive income by increasing their base of loyal and satisfied customers.

There are several websites and applications that use sentiment analysis to generate passive income.

Here are a few examples:

- **Hootsuite Insights:** This social media analytics platform uses AI to analyze online conversations and determine how customers perceive a brand or product.

- **Mention:** This social media monitoring app also uses AI to analyze online conversations and provide insights into brand reputation and customer satisfaction.

- **Sprout Social:** This social media management platform uses sentiment analysis to monitor online conversations and provide insights into customer perceptions.

- **IBM Watson:** This data analytics platform uses AI sentiment analysis to provide information on customer perception and market trends.

- **Brandwatch:** This social media monitoring platform uses AI to monitor online conversations and provide insights into brand reputation and customer satisfaction.

- **Talkwalker**: This social media analytics and monitoring platform offers real-time insights into brand reputation, customer sentiment, and industry trends.

- **ReviewTrackers:** This platform tracks online reviews and customer feedback from multiple sources to help businesses improve their reputation and customer satisfaction.

- **Medallia:** This customer experience management platform uses AI-powered sentiment analysis to identify customer issues and opportunities for improvement.

Overall, sentiment analysis is a powerful tool for businesses to improve their customer experience and reputation, leading to increased revenue and customer loyalty. These tools can help businesses improve their online reputation, quickly respond to customer issues, and make more informed marketing decisions.

AI-Powered Voice Optimization for Your Website

Using AI to optimize your website for voice search and improve your search engine ranking.

With the growing popularity of voice assistants such as Alexa and Siri, voice search optimization has become an important online marketing strategy for businesses.

By using natural language processing powered by AI, companies can tailor their website and content to address frequently asked questions by voice search users.

By optimizing for voice search, businesses can increase their online visibility and attract more traffic to their website.

This is because voice search results are often more concise and to-the-point than text search results, meaning users are more likely to click on the first results presented. Moreover,

by using natural keywords and focusing on common questions by voice search users, businesses can improve their search engine rankings, which can increase their online visibility and generate more traffic.

Ultimately, voice search optimization can be an effective online marketing strategy for businesses looking to increase their online visibility and generate passive income by attracting more traffic to their website.

Here are 10 applications and websites that can help generate revenue by optimizing for voice search:

- **Google Search Console:** This Google platform allows you to track the performance of your website and identify the keywords used to access it.

- **AnswerThePublic:** This application provides information on the most frequently asked questions on a particular topic, which can help identify the key terms to use for voice search.

- **SEMrush:** This application provides data on keywords, rankings, and content strategies to improve natural referencing and voice search.

- **Yoast SEO:** This WordPress extension helps optimize website content for voice search and search engines.

- **Amazon Alexa Skills Kit:** This platform allows businesses to create Alexa skills for their products and services, increasing their visibility among Alexa users.

- **Jovo:** This application allows businesses to create Alexa and Google Assistant skills to improve voice search.

Dialogflow: This Google platform allows you to create conversational agents for voice assistants, allowing for more advanced interaction with users.

BotStar: This application allows businesses to create chatbots for voice assistants, increasing interaction with customers.

Voiceflow: This application allows businesses to create conversation workflows for voice assistants, allowing for smoother interaction with users.

Cerence: This platform allows businesses to create high-quality virtual assistants for cars and other devices, increasing interaction with customers while on-the-go.

Image recognition is an AI-powered technology that enables the analysis of images to identify products and services.

With this technology, businesses can recommend similar products based on visual characteristics of a product.

This technique can generate passive revenue by increasing the probability of a sale and improving the customer experience. In fact, image recognition can be used to enhance the online shopping experience by helping customers find products similar to what they are looking for, even if they do not know the exact name of the product.

Using sophisticated algorithms, image recognition can also recommend complementary products based on the visual characteristics of a product. This technology is particularly useful for e-commerce businesses as it can recommend relevant and high-quality products to customers, which can increase sales and customer satisfaction.

Furthermore, image recognition can also help businesses improve their SEO by using accurate product descriptions and images optimized for search engines.

Ultimately, AI-powered image recognition is a powerful technique to help businesses increase their revenue and improve the customer experience. Businesses can use this technology to identify products and services, recommend similar products, and improve their SEO, which can lead to an increase in sales and customer loyalty.

Here are websites and applications that can help entrepreneurs generate revenue through image recognition:

- **Slyce** - an image recognition platform that allows users to take a picture of a product and receive recommendations for similar products.

- **Google Lens** - an image recognition app developed by Google that allows users to take a picture of a product and receive detailed information about the product.

- **Amazon Rekognition** - an Amazon Web Services image recognition service that allows businesses to detect and analyze objects and scenes in images.

- **Clarifai** - an image recognition platform that uses AI to analyze images and videos and classify them based on their content.

- **Visenze** - an image recognition platform that allows businesses to create product catalogs and recommend similar products based on visual characteristics.

- **Pinterest Lens** - an image recognition feature on Pinterest that allows users to take a picture of a product and receive recommendations for similar products on Pinterest.

- **ViSenze** - a company that offers AI-based visual search technology to help e-commerce businesses recommend similar products to their customers.

- **TinEye** - a reverse image search engine that allows users to find the origin of an image or find similar images on the web.

Maximizing Profits with Dynamic Pricing

Dynamic pricing is a pricing technique that involves adjusting the prices of products and services in real-time based on various factors such as market demand, supply, and competition.

This strategy is becoming increasingly popular in e-commerce, hospitality, airline industries, and many other sectors.

The integration of Artificial Intelligence (AI) in dynamic pricing has allowed for even more automation of the pricing adjustment process.

AI algorithms can collect and analyze large amounts of real-time data, such as conversion rates, click-through rates, customer buying behaviors, weather data, and other external factors, to determine the optimal price.

AI-powered dynamic pricing allows businesses to adapt their prices to fluctuations in market demand, increasing or decreasing prices based on trends and customer buying behaviors. This can help businesses maximize their revenue by selling products and services at the highest possible price without deterring potential customers.

This strategy can generate passive income by optimizing the prices of products and services, which can lead to increased sales and profit margins.

Additionally, AI-powered dynamic pricing can also help retain customers by offering competitive and personalized pricing.

Ultimately, AI-powered dynamic pricing is an increasingly common technique to help businesses maximize their revenue and improve customer experience. Sophisticated AI algorithms can help businesses adjust prices in real-time based on market demand and other factors, leading to increased sales, profit margins, and customer loyalty.

Here are 10 websites and applications that can help entrepreneurs generate revenue through dynamic pricing:

- **Dynamic Pricing** - a dynamic pricing platform for e-commerce sites that automatically adjusts prices in real-time based on demand. .

- **PriceLabs** - a dynamic pricing tool for vacation rentals that uses AI to adjust prices based on demand, competition, and other factors.

- Beyond Pricing - a dynamic pricing platform for vacation rentals that automatically adjusts prices based on market demand.

- **Revionics** - a dynamic pricing solution for retailers that uses AI to adjust prices based on demand, competition, and other factors.

- **Prisync** - a price tracking tool that uses AI to help businesses adjust prices based on market demand and competition.

- **Incompetitor** - a competition tracking platform that uses AI to help businesses adjust prices in real-time based on competition.

- **Omnia Retail** - a dynamic pricing platform for retailers that uses AI to adjust prices based on demand, competition, and other factors.

- **Wiser** - a dynamic pricing solution for retailers that uses AI to adjust prices based on demand, competition, and other factors.

- **Quicklizard** - a dynamic pricing platform for e-commerce sites that uses AI to adjust prices in real-time based on demand.

- **Competera** - a dynamic pricing solution for retailers that uses AI to adjust prices based on demand, competition, and other factors.

A.Explanation of the role of AI in healthcare.

Artificial intelligence (AI) is playing an increasingly important role in the healthcare field. Indeed, AI allows for the processing and analysis of large amounts of medical data in record time, which can help healthcare professionals make more informed decisions and improve the quality of care. Among the applications of AI in healthcare, we can mention:

Medical image analysis: AI can be used to analyze medical images, such as X-rays or scans, to help doctors detect anomalies or diseases. This analysis can be faster and more accurate than human analysis.

Diagnosis and treatment: AI can be used to help diagnose diseases by analyzing medical data and comparing the patient's symptoms to a database of medical knowledge. AI can also help recommend personalized treatments based on patient data.

Patient monitoring: AI can be used to monitor patients remotely, by analyzing sensor data, vital signs, and health data collected using wearable devices. This can help healthcare professionals detect early signs of disease and intervene quickly.

Improving medical research: AI can be used to help speed up medical research by analyzing large amounts of medical data and identifying patterns and trends.

Overall, AI can help healthcare professionals improve patient care, reduce medical errors, and accelerate medical research.

B.Generating passive income in the healthcare industry with AI: 10 essential methods!

Revolutionizing Healthcare: AI-powered Method for Passive Income through Telemedicine

Telemedicine is a method of remote healthcare that uses communication technologies to connect patients with healthcare professionals.

AI can play an important role in telemedicine by helping diagnose diseases and recommending personalized treatments based on patient data.

Here are the steps to generate passive income in the field of telemedicine using AI:

- Identify a niche: It is important to find a specific niche in telemedicine to differentiate from the competition. For example, specialize in teleradiology or tele-mental health.

- Set up an online platform: Create an online platform to offer telemedicine services. The platform should be user-friendly and allow patients to schedule appointments online and communicate with healthcare professionals.

- Integrate AI: Integrate AI into the platform to help diagnose diseases and recommend personalized treatments based on patient data. For example, use a machine learning algorithm to analyze patients' medical data and provide treatment recommendations.

- Hire healthcare professionals: Hire healthcare professionals to provide remote care to patients. Healthcare professionals must be licensed to practice in the state where the online platform is located.

- Advertise: Promote the online platform to attract patients. Use online marketing techniques such as SEO, online ads, and social media.

- Bill patients: Bill patients for telemedicine services. Fees can be based on consultation time or type of service offered.

In summary, telemedicine is a method of remote healthcare that can be profitable by using AI to diagnose diseases and recommend personalized treatments. Key steps to generate passive income in telemedicine include identifying a niche, creating an online platform, integrating AI, hiring healthcare professionals, advertising, and billing patients.

Mental health: AI as a diagnostic and treatment tool.

The use of AI in the field of mental health can offer significant benefits for patients. Firstly, it can help to quickly and accurately diagnose mental disorders such as depression, anxiety, and post-traumatic stress disorder.

Using sophisticated algorithms, AI can analyze a patient's symptoms and history to determine a more precise diagnosis than would be possible with human evaluation alone.

Additionally, AI can provide personalized advice and suggestions to help patients manage their mental health. By using data on the patient's lifestyle habits and behaviors, AI can provide recommendations on nutrition, exercise, and other healthy habits that can help improve mood and reduce stress. It can also suggest personalized therapies based on the specific needs of the patient.

Finally, the use of AI in mental health can also make treatment more affordable and accessible. Patients can benefit from online or remote treatment, avoiding travel costs and time constraints. This can also help reduce wait times for an appointment with a mental health professional.

There are several ways to generate passive income in the field of mental health through the use of AI:

- Develop and sell AI mobile apps for mental health management: Mobile apps can use AI to provide personalized advice and stress management techniques to users, and these apps can be sold for passive income.

- Create and sell online coaching programs: AI can be used to help provide personalized advice through online coaching programs for mental health management. Users can subscribe to these programs for passive income.

- Sell wellness products online: Wellness products such as nutritional supplements, essential oils, and relaxation devices can be sold online with the help of AI to target customers interested in mental health and wellness.

- Create online courses on mental health: Online courses can be created to help people learn stress and mental health management techniques. These courses can be sold online for passive income.

- Offer online counseling services: Mental health counselors can offer online counseling services using AI to diagnose mental disorders and provide personalized advice. These services can be offered for passive income.

By using AI to improve mental health services, it is possible to create sources of passive income while helping people manage their mental health.

Generating passive income in the healthcare industry through the development of an effective chatbot

The development of a healthcare chatbot is an innovative and effective method to improve healthcare efficiency through AI.

Healthcare chatbots can provide quick responses and personalized advice to patients, which can help reduce staffing costs while still offering quality service to patients.

One of the main reasons why healthcare chatbots are so popular is that they can answer patient questions 24/7 without interruption. This means that patients can get immediate answers to their questions even outside of normal clinic and hospital hours.

Healthcare chatbots also use machine learning to provide personalized advice and solutions to patients. As a result, they can be more accurate than human healthcare professionals who have to handle many different patients at the same time.

Finally, healthcare chatbots are very cost-effective. They are less expensive than human healthcare professionals and can answer a large number of questions at the same time. This helps reduce staffing costs while improving healthcare quality.

The development of a healthcare chatbot can be an effective method to generate passive income in the healthcare industry with AI. Here's how to proceed:

- Define the chatbot's objectives: Before starting to develop your chatbot, clearly define the objectives you want to achieve. What services will the chatbot offer to patients and what problems will it solve? Also think about the types of questions the chatbot will need to answer.

- Collect data: To develop an effective healthcare chatbot, you need accurate and complete data. Collect data on symptoms, diseases, treatments, and medications. You can obtain this data from healthcare professionals, public databases, or other reliable sources.

- Choose a chatbot platform: There are many chatbot platforms available on the market. Choose a platform that suits your specific needs for development and integration. Some platforms offer additional features such as machine learning and voice recognition.

- Design the chatbot's dialogue: Dialogue is crucial to the success of a healthcare chatbot. Design clear and user-friendly dialogue using simple and understandable terms for patients. Test the dialogue with real patients to evaluate its effectiveness and make necessary adjustments.

- Integrate AI: Healthcare chatbots use AI to provide quick and personalized responses to patients. Integrate machine learning technology to improve the accuracy and efficiency of the chatbot. The more the chatbot is used, the smarter it will become and the better it will be able to answer complex questions.

- Test and refine the chatbot: Test your chatbot on a small group of patients before deploying it on a larger scale. Evaluate the chatbot's performance in terms of response accuracy, response time, and user satisfaction. Make necessary adjustments to improve user experience.

Once your healthcare chatbot is operational, you can market it to doctors, hospitals, and other healthcare professionals to generate long-term passive income

Investing in Healthcare Startups

Investing in healthcare startups can be a lucrative opportunity to generate long-term passive income. Thanks to advances in AI, healthcare startups are rapidly growing and can offer innovative solutions to improve the quality of healthcare.

By investing in healthcare startups, you can obtain significant returns on your investment while also contributing to improving patients' lives. Healthcare startups are working on projects such as early disease detection, electronic medical record management, telemedicine, personalized therapies, and much more.

Additionally, investing in healthcare startups can provide tax benefits such as tax credits for investments in startup companies. These benefits can significantly reduce your tax burden and increase your return on investment. However, it is important to understand that investing in healthcare startups also comes with risks. Startups often have limited funds to finance their projects and may face unforeseen challenges such as strict regulations or fierce competition. Therefore, it is important to conduct thorough research on each startup before investing.

The steps to successfully invest in healthcare startups are as follows:

- Conduct research: It is important to conduct thorough research on healthcare startups before investing. You need to understand their business model, leadership team, vision and mission, as well as the challenges they face.

- Define your investment strategy: You need to determine the goal of your investment, the amount you are willing to invest, and the type of startup that best fits your investment portfolio.

- Choose an online investment platform: There are several online investment platforms for healthcare startups. Some popular platforms include AngelList, SeedInvest, and OurCrowd.

- Evaluate startups: Online investment platforms provide information about startups available for investment. You can use this information to evaluate startups based on their funding history, growth potential, and leadership team.

- Select startups to invest in: After evaluating startups, you can select those that best fit your investment strategy and invest in them.

It is also important to note that you can engage a financial advisor to assist you in this process

Reduce the Risk of Diseases with AI-Driven Prevention Services for Better Health

Offering prevention services to your clients can be an excellent way to improve their health and grow your business. Prevention services help clients identify potential risks of diseases and conditions before they develop, and provide guidance on how to reduce these risks.

Integrating AI into prevention services can be particularly useful in predicting individual disease risks. AI can analyze client health data such as medical histories, dietary habits, and levels of physical activity to identify potential disease risks. By using this information, you can develop a personalized plan to help the client reduce their risk of contracting a specific disease or condition.

Prevention services may also include personalized exercise and nutrition programs tailored to the client's specific needs. These programs can be designed with the help of a qualified healthcare professional such as a nutritionist or personal trainer, to help the client achieve their health goals.

By offering prevention services to your clients, you can also strengthen the relationship between your business and your clients. Clients see that you care about their overall health and well-being, which can increase their loyalty to your business

There are several methods to generate passive income by offering prevention services to your clients. Here are some of the methods and applications/software you can use:

- **Personalized meal planning** - You can use apps such as MyFitnessPal, Mealime, or Yummly to create personalized meal plans for your clients.

- **Custom exercise programs** - Apps such as Fitbod, Nike Training Club, and Freeletics can be used to create custom exercise programs for your clients.

- **Health monitoring** - Apps such as HealthTap, Medici, and Lemonaid can be used to monitor your clients' health status and provide advice on maintaining good health.

- **Online health coaching** - You can use platforms such as Coach.me, BetterHelp, or Noom to provide online health coaching services to your clients.

- **Using AI to predict disease risks** - You can use software such as IBM Watson Health or Google DeepMind to analyze your clients' health data and identify potential disease risks.

By using these methods and tools, you can offer prevention services to your clients and generate passive income while helping them improve their health and well-being.

Create an AI Mobile Health Application to Generate Passive Income

The creation of a mobile health application can be an excellent opportunity to generate passive income. Health mobile apps are booming and offer features such as calorie tracking, sleep tracking, and fitness tracking.

By using AI to develop key features, you can enhance the user experience and offer more personalized services. For example, AI can help analyze user health data to provide personalized recommendations on nutrition and exercise.

Calorie tracking is an essential feature in many health apps. Users can input their daily food consumption and get information on nutrients, calories, and macros. AI can be used to improve calorie tracking by providing personalized suggestions on foods or recipes that match each user's nutritional preferences and needs.

Sleep tracking is another popular feature in health apps. Users can track their sleep to determine if they are getting enough rest and receive advice on improving sleep quality. By using AI, you can provide deeper analyses of the user's sleep and suggest behavior changes to improve their sleep quality.

Fitness tracking is another feature that can be enhanced through AI. Users can track their progress in fitness and receive advice on reaching their goals. AI can be used to analyze user data and provide personalized recommendations to help them reach their fitness goals faster.

In addition to the previously mentioned features, there are numerous other features that you can offer in your mobile health application to enhance the user experience and generate passive income. For example, you can provide online training programs with explanatory videos and advice from fitness professionals. You can also include a goal tracking feature to help users achieve their health and wellness goals.

Furthermore, you can offer exclusive content such as healthy recipes, nutrition and fitness tips, as well as guides on stress management and mental health. This exclusive content can be accessed through monthly or yearly subscription fees, which can serve as an additional source of revenue for your mobile health application.

It is important to keep in mind that competition in the mobile health app industry is fierce. To stand out from the competition, it is crucial to offer an exceptional user experience and innovative features that meet consumers' health and wellness needs.

Finally, don't forget to promote your mobile health app using appropriate marketing channels such as social media, paid advertising, and public relations. By making your app known to the public, you can attract new users and generate even more passive income

The Power of Personalization: How AI is Transforming Wellness Programs

Wellness programs are sets of activities aimed at improving a person's health and well-being. These programs can include a variety of elements such as meditation exercises, yoga classes, nutritional advice, relaxation techniques, and more.

The advantage of these programs is that they can be customized to meet the individual needs of each client. By using AI, it is possible to collect data on clients such as their age, level of physical fitness, dietary habits, and mental health. AI can then use this information to customize wellness programs based on the specific needs of each client.

For example, if a client suffers from stress and anxiety, AI can recommend meditation and deep breathing activities to help reduce stress levels and improve mood. If a client needs to improve their physical condition, AI can recommend yoga or cardio exercises tailored to their fitness level.

Here are 10 AI-based methods to generate passive income with wellness programs:

- Create a wellness chatbot: You can create a wellness chatbot that can help users find personalized advice on health and wellness. You can integrate AI algorithms to offer contextually relevant suggestions.

- Use data analytics to personalize wellness programs: By using in-depth data analytics, you can personalize wellness programs for each user based on their preferences and goals.

- Develop an AI-powered wellness application: You can develop an AI-powered wellness application that can help users track their physical activity, nutrition, and sleep. The app can provide personalized suggestions to improve health and wellness.

- Offer AI-powered virtual coaching services: You can offer AI-powered virtual coaching services where the AI can help users achieve their wellness goals. Users can interact with the AI via a chat or video conferencing platform.

- Use machine learning to predict health behaviors: By using machine learning, you can analyze user health data and predict their future behavior. Based on these predictions, you can offer personalized suggestions to improve health and wellness.

- Provide AI-based meditation programs: You can offer AI-based meditation programs that can help users find a state of relaxation and calm. The AI can suggest personalized meditation techniques based on each user's preferences.

- Create AI-powered nutrition chatbots: You can create AI-powered nutrition chatbots that can offer personalized advice for healthy eating. The chatbots can analyze user eating habits and provide tailored suggestions to meet their needs.

- Use voice recognition to control wellness applications: You can use voice recognition to allow users to control wellness applications with their voices. This can make the app easier and more convenient to use.

- Build an AI-based exercise recommendation system: Using machine learning, you can create an exercise recommendation system based on user preferences and goals. The system can suggest personalized exercises based on the user's physical abilities.

- Offer AI-based mental coaching services: You can use AI to detect signs of stress or anxiety in users and offer personalized advice to improve their mental health. These coaching services can be offered through an app or chatbot platform.

Clinical decision support systems based on AI are software that use machine learning and data analysis to help physicians make more informed treatment decisions.

The process of developing such a system involves several stages:

Data collection: The first step is to collect the necessary data to train the system. This data can include medical records, laboratory data, medical images, test results, and other relevant information.

Data preprocessing: The collected data needs to be preprocessed to remove errors, missing data, and irrelevant data. The data also needs to be normalized to ensure the quality of input data.

Model training: The AI model needs to be trained on preprocessed data to learn the relationships between different variables and identify key features associated with different treatments. This step can take time and requires significant computing power.

Model validation: Once the model is trained, it needs to be validated to ensure its accuracy and reliability. This involves testing the model on a separate dataset to check its performance.

Integration into a clinical decision support system: Once the model is validated, it can be integrated into a clinical decision support system. This system can be designed to help physicians make a diagnosis, choose the best treatment, monitor patients, and adjust treatment based on results.

Once the clinical decision support system is developed, it can be sold to healthcare facilities to help physicians make more informed treatment decisions. Companies can offer subscription models for the use of their clinical decision support systems, thereby generating passive revenue.

The method of generating passive income from AI-based appointment scheduling systems involves several steps:

Development of the appointment scheduling system: The first step is to develop an AI-based appointment scheduling system that can help healthcare facilities efficiently manage their appointments. This system can be designed to schedule appointments, send reminders to patients, manage cancellations and rescheduling, and provide data analysis reports on system performance.

Integration with healthcare facilities: Once the appointment scheduling system is developed, it needs to be integrated with healthcare facilities to allow patients to schedule appointments online. This integration may require the implementation of security protocols to ensure the confidentiality of medical information.

Marketing the appointment scheduling system: Companies can market their appointment scheduling system to healthcare facilities. They can offer monthly or annual subscription models for the use of their system, which generates regular passive income.

Maintenance and updating of the system: The appointment scheduling system must be regularly maintained and updated to ensure its proper functioning and security. This may involve bug fixes, feature improvements, and updating security protocols.

In summary, selling AI-based appointment scheduling systems can generate passive income for companies, while also providing a practical and efficient solution for healthcare facilities in managing their appointments.

Selling AI-based patient monitoring systems can be a source of passive income for companies specializing in health technology. This type of system allows healthcare facilities to remotely monitor patients, improving their quality of care and operational efficiency.

The process of generating passive income from AI-based patient monitoring systems may include the following steps:

System development: The first step is to develop an AI-based patient monitoring system that can help healthcare facilities monitor their patients remotely. This system may include wearable sensors, home monitoring devices, and mobile applications.

Integration with healthcare facilities: Once the system is developed, it must be integrated into healthcare facilities to allow for remote patient monitoring. This step may involve implementing security protocols to ensure the confidentiality of medical information

Marketing the patient monitoring system: Companies can market their patient monitoring system to healthcare facilities. They can offer monthly or yearly subscription models for the use of their system, thereby generating regular passive income.

System maintenance and updates: The patient monitoring system must be regularly maintained and updated to ensure its proper functioning and security. This may involve bug fixes, feature improvements, and security protocol updates.

AI-based patient monitoring systems can offer a practical and effective solution for improving the quality of care and operational efficiency of healthcare facilities. Companies specializing in health technology can generate regular passive income by selling this type of system.

The 10 Passive Income Methods Related to Artificial Intelligence in the Education Field

A. Explanation of the Role of AI in Education.

Artificial intelligence (AI) is increasingly being used in the field of education to improve students' learning experience and help teachers provide more personalized instruction.

With recent technological advancements, AI is capable of processing large amounts of data, analyzing patterns, and providing real-time information. These capabilities are particularly useful in education, where teachers have to process a lot of information about their students and provide accurate assessments of their performance.

AI systems can help manage courses by automating certain tasks such as attendance tracking, homework collection and grading, and organizing class schedules. This can save teachers time and energy, allowing them to focus on teaching and interacting with students.

AI can also help provide more personalized instruction. AI systems can identify students' knowledge gaps and provide them with additional resources to help them progress. For example, if a student struggles with math, an AI system can provide additional resources to help them understand fundamental concepts.

AI systems can also recommend additional educational resources such as videos, articles, and books based on each student's learning preferences. AI systems can use machine learning to analyze each student's learning patterns and recommend resources that best suit their learning style.

Finally, AI can be used to analyze student performance and predict their future performance. AI systems can use machine learning algorithms to analyze students' learning patterns and predict their future performance based on their past performance. These predictions can help teachers adapt their teaching approach to better meet each student's needs.

In summary, AI can have a significant impact on the field of education by improving students' learning experiences and helping teachers provide more personalized instruction. AI systems can help manage courses, automatically grade assignments, recommend educational resources, and analyze student performance, allowing teachers to focus on teaching and interacting with students.

B.Presenting 10 Passive Income Methods in the Education Field.

Sale of educational AI software

Selling educational AI software can be a lucrative method for generating passive income. Here are some tips for developing and selling educational AI software:

Identify needs: Before starting to develop educational AI software, it's important to understand the needs of students and teachers. AI software can be used to improve learning and teaching in many subjects, so by identifying specific needs, you can create more useful and attractive software.

Choose a development platform: There are several AI software development platforms available, such as TensorFlow, PyTorch, or Keras. Choosing the right platform is important to ensure the quality and efficiency of the software.

Recruit talented developers: The quality of the software largely depends on the developers' skills. Therefore, recruiting talented developers is essential to creating effective and high-performing software.

Test and refine the software: It's important to test and refine the software before launching it on the market. Testing ensures that the software is effective and that users can easily use it.

Find sales channels: Once the software is ready to be sold, it's important to find effective sales channels to reach potential customers. Sales channels can include online platforms, partnerships with schools and businesses, or targeted advertising campaigns.

Regarding the necessary software for developing educational AI software, it will depend on the chosen platform and the software's features. AI software often requires programming languages such as Python or R, as well as tools such as deep learning libraries or AI frameworks. It's important to research to find the most suitable software for your needs.

Creating and selling educational content online: Companies can create and sell AI-based online courses, such as programming or foreign language courses, for passive income.

To create and sell AI-based online courses, here are some steps and software to use:

Determine the subject and target audience: Before starting to create online courses, it's important to determine the subject and target audience. You can use market research tools such as Google Trends or Keyword Planner to find popular and in-demand topic ideas.

Create the content: To create high-quality content, you can use online course creation software such as Udemy, Teachable, or Coursera. These platforms offer tools to create videos, presentations, quizzes, discussion forums, etc.

Use AI tools to enhance learning: To enhance your students' learning, you can use AI tools such as speech recognition for language courses, chatbots to answer student questions, or recommendation tools to suggest complementary courses.

Set up a sales platform: To sell your online courses, you can use online sales platforms such as Udemy, Teachable, or Shopify. These platforms allow you to create an online store to sell your courses and manage payments and registrations.

Use digital marketing to promote your courses: To reach a wider audience, use digital marketing strategies such as online advertising, email marketing, and social media to promote your courses.

In terms of necessary software, you can use content creation tools such as Adobe Premiere for video creation, Canva for presentation and infographic creation, and Hootsuite for social media management. For AI tools, you can use AI APIs such as Google Cloud AI or IBM Watson to add AI features to your online courses.

Selling AI training services

Selling AI training services has become a booming industry as more and more businesses seek to integrate AI into their teaching and training. Companies offering these services can help schools and businesses understand the basics of AI, the tools and techniques necessary to integrate AI into their programs, and best practices for using AI effectively.

AI training services can be offered in various ways, such as online courses, on-site training, seminars, workshops, etc. Companies that offer these services can also customize their training programs based on the specific needs of their clients.

To offer AI training services, companies need qualified and experienced personnel in the field of AI. They must also have the necessary tools and technologies to provide high-quality training services. Companies can use tools such as AI simulators, machine learning software, natural language processing systems, etc.

In terms of marketing these services, companies can use digital marketing strategies such as online advertising, email marketing, and social media to reach a wider audience. They can also participate in industry events to showcase their AI training services and meet potential clients.

Overall, selling AI training services can be a lucrative business for companies that have the expertise and resources to offer high-quality training services. As the benefits of AI become increasingly evident, it is likely that demand for these services will continue to grow in the future.

The sales process to generate revenue from selling AI training services may include the following steps:

Identifying the target market: First, the company must identify the target market for its AI training services. This may include schools, universities, businesses, government and non-profit organizations, or any other entity interested in integrating AI into its education and training.

Developing a service offer: The company must develop a clear and comprehensive service offer that describes the AI training services it provides, the benefits of these services, the training modalities, costs, and durations. The service offer should be tailored to the specific needs of each potential client.

Prospecting: The company must prospect to find potential clients interested in its AI training services. This may include sending emails, participating in industry events, online advertising, or direct prospecting.

Presenting the offer: Once the company has found potential clients, it must arrange an offer presentation to explain in detail the AI training services it offers, the benefits of these services, the training modalities, costs, and durations.

Negotiation: After the offer presentation, the company may be called upon to negotiate with potential clients to finalize the training modalities, including costs and durations.

Contract signing: Once the training modalities are agreed upon, the company and potential client must sign a contract describing the AI training services and the training modalities.

Providing AI training services: Once the contract is signed, the company can provide the AI training services, including online training, in-person training, seminars, workshops, etc.

Invoicing and payment: At the end of the training, the company must invoice the client for the AI training services provided. Payment may be made in installments depending on the payment terms agreed upon in the contract.

The process to generate passive income from creating and selling educational chatbots can include the following steps:

Identify the target market: First, it is important to identify the target market for educational chatbots, such as students at different education levels, teachers, parents, or educational institutions.

Design and develop educational chatbots: Once the target market is identified, the educational chatbots must be designed and developed using AI and natural language processing technologies. The chatbots should be personalized to meet the specific needs of target users, such as common questions and problems.

Test the educational chatbots: Once the educational chatbots are developed, they must be tested to ensure they effectively answer questions and solve problems. Testing can be done internally or in collaboration with educational partners to obtain feedback from potential users.

Market the educational chatbots: After the testing phase, the educational chatbots must be marketed using channels such as social media, websites, online selling platforms, partnerships with educational institutions, etc. The chatbots should be presented as a practical and effective solution to help students learn and solve problems.

Sell the educational chatbots: When potential clients express interest, the terms of the sale, including payment terms, usage rights, future updates, etc., must be negotiated. Once the terms are agreed upon, the educational chatbots must be delivered to the client.

Follow-up and technical assistance: It is important to provide follow-up and technical assistance to clients to ensure the chatbots work properly and meet the needs of users.

Passive income: After the initial sale, educational chatbots can continue to generate passive income for the company using pricing models such as subscriptions, licenses, or one-time purchases. The chatbots must be regularly updated to remain relevant and meet the needs of users.

The method of selling educational AI games involves developing educational games using AI technologies to help students learn in a fun and interactive way. AI educational games can take different forms, such as quizzes, simulations, role-playing games, etc., and can be adapted to different levels of education and different learning subjects.

To implement this method, companies must first identify the target market for AI educational games, such as schools, teachers, parents, or students themselves. Then, they must design and develop the games using AI technologies such as voice recognition, natural language understanding, and machine learning to create an engaging and interactive learning experience.

The software that can be used to develop AI-based educational games includes game development tools such as Unity, Unreal Engine, and Construct. It may also be necessary to use natural language processing and machine learning tools to integrate AI into games.

The process for developing and selling AI-based educational games may include the following steps:

Identify the target market: It is important to define the target audience for the educational games, such as children of specific ages or students at a certain level of education.

Design the educational games: The games must be designed using pedagogical principles to ensure that they are educational while remaining fun. AI elements can be integrated to enhance the gaming experience, such as customizing the content based on the user's skills.

Develop the educational games: The games must be developed using appropriate software to ensure that they are interactive and user-friendly. AI elements must be seamlessly integrated into the game.

Test the educational games: Once the games are developed, they need to be tested to ensure that they are educational and function properly. Testing can be done internally or in collaboration with educational partners to get feedback from potential users.

Market the educational games: The educational games need to be marketed using channels such as social media, websites, online selling platforms, partnerships with educational institutions, etc. The games should be presented as a practical and effective solution to help students learn in a fun way.

Sell the educational games: When potential customers show interest, the terms of the sale, including payment terms, usage rights, future updates, etc., need to be negotiated. Once the terms are accepted, the educational games need to be provided to the customer.

Follow-up and technical support: It is important to provide follow-up and technical support to customers to ensure that the games work properly and meet the needs of the users.

Creating an AI-based online research platform involves setting up a system capable of analyzing and sorting a large number of information sources to provide students and teachers with relevant results for their research.
The process may include the following steps:

- **Collecting information sources** - It is necessary to collect a wide range of information sources such as research articles, books, journals, theses, and dissertations. Sources can be collected from online databases, university libraries, government and non-governmental organization websites, etc.

- **Indexing sources** - The collected sources must be indexed and categorized by subject and domain to facilitate later searching.

- **Using AI for analysis and research** - Once the sources are indexed, AI can be used to analyze the content of each source and identify relevant topics, keywords, and themes. The analysis results can be used to sort and categorize the sources according to their relevance for a particular research.

- **Providing results** - The research results can be presented to platform users in the form of lists of sources sorted by relevance, with summaries, excerpts, or links to the complete sources.

There are several sites and tools that can be used to create an AI-based online research platform. Some of these tools include Google Scholar, Microsoft Academic, Semantic Scholar, and OpenAI's GPT-3. These tools can be used to collect, index, and analyze information sources to present them to users in a relevant manner. Development tools such as Python, Django, and Flask can be used to create the platform's user interface.

Creating a virtual teacher using the DID website to generate educational videos can be a great way to generate passive income in the education industry.

The process can include the following steps:

Setting up an account with DID website - The first step is to create an account with DID website, which provides a platform for creating animated videos with virtual characters.

Creating a virtual teacher - Using the website's tools and resources, you can create a virtual teacher that can be customized to fit your preferences. You can choose the teacher's appearance, voice, and behavior to make it more engaging and relevant to your audience.

Writing scripts and recording voiceovers - Once the virtual teacher is created, you need to write scripts for the educational videos and record voiceovers that will be used to bring the teacher to life. The scripts should be informative and engaging, with clear explanations of complex concepts.

Designing the video content - The DID website provides tools for designing and creating the video content, including animations, graphics, and other visual aids. You can use these tools to make the videos more interesting and informative for your audience.

Publishing the videos - Once the videos are created, you can publish them on YouTube or other educational websites to reach a wider audience. You can also monetize the videos through advertising, sponsorships, or other revenue-generating strategies.

Overall, creating a virtual teacher using the DID website can be an effective way to generate passive income in the education industry. By creating informative and engaging educational videos, you can build a loyal following of students and educators who value your expertise and insights.

To create an online mentoring platform based on AI, there are several steps to follow:

Define the platform's objectives and functionalities: To begin, it is important to determine the objectives of the platform and the functionalities it must have to meet the needs of mentors and students. For example, the platform can offer matching tools based on the interests and skills of students and mentors, communication tools to facilitate exchanges, resources to help mentors and students achieve their goals, and evaluation tools to measure progress.

Collect data: To power the AI, it is important to collect data on mentors and students. This may include information on their academic background, interests, skills, and career goals. It may also be useful to collect data on interactions between mentors and students, such as messages exchanged and projects completed together.

Set up the AI: The AI used on the platform must be capable of analyzing the collected data and providing matching recommendations based on the interests and skills of mentors and students. It must also be able to track students' progress and provide recommendations to help them achieve their goals.

Develop the user interface: The platform's user interface must be easy to use and intuitive. Students and mentors should be able to create profiles, search for mentors/students, communicate easily, and access resources.

Test and refine the platform: It is important to test the platform with a small group of mentors and students to ensure that it meets their needs. User feedback can be used to improve the platform and make it more effective.

Develop an automatic translation tool that uses AI to translate courses and educational resources into different languages. This tool can help make education more accessible to a wider audience.

Defining the Target Audience: It is important to determine the target audience for your automatic translation tool. Students and online learners are an obvious target, but it can also be useful to target teachers and educators who are looking to make their materials more accessible to an international audience.

Collecting Data and Training the AI: To develop a quality automatic translation tool, it is important to collect data and use it to train the AI. This can include texts in different languages, educational documents, audio and video recordings of courses, and human translations to help improve accuracy.

Designing the User Interface: The user interface of the automatic translation tool should be easy to use and intuitive. Users should be able to upload documents or enter text in different languages and select the destination language. The tool should then provide accurate real-time translation.

Setting up the Website: To generate revenue, you can create a website for your automatic translation tool. You can offer limited free access to the tool to attract users, but you can also offer a premium subscription for unlimited access to all the features of the tool.

Monetizing the Translation Tool: You can generate revenue using different strategies, such as targeted advertising for tool users, selling premium subscriptions, or selling anonymized usage data to third parties interested in information about users and their learning habits.

The emotion recognition tool

The emotion recognition tool is a promising method to help teachers assess students' understanding and engagement during online classes. Here's how to develop this method:

Collect data: To develop an effective emotion recognition tool, it's important to collect quality data. Data can be collected from cameras, microphones, and motion sensors to track students' movements. The data can include facial expressions, vocal intonations, and body movements. This data is used to train the AI to recognize students' different emotions.

Train the AI: The AI must be trained to recognize students' different emotions, such as confusion, boredom, interest, excitement, frustration, etc. To do this, the collected data must be annotated to indicate which emotion is associated with each action.

Design the user interface: The user interface of the emotion recognition tool should be easy to use for teachers. The tool should provide accurate information about students' emotions in real-time to help teachers adapt their teaching approach. The interface should also be user-friendly so that teachers can easily navigate and access different features of the tool.

Test and refine the tool: Once the emotion recognition tool has been developed, it must be tested to evaluate its accuracy and effectiveness. Tests should be conducted in different online class environments to ensure that the tool works properly. Results should be used to refine and improve the tool.

Monetize the emotion recognition tool: To generate revenue, you can offer limited free access to the tool to attract users, but you can also offer a premium subscription for unlimited access to all the tool's features. You can also consider selling anonymized usage data to interested third parties for information about students and their emotions during online classes.

Conclusion

This book provides an exciting opportunity for entrepreneurs by presenting the various ways in which artificial intelligence can be used to generate passive income in different fields. The 50 methods presented offer a source of inspiration for individuals looking to leverage AI while pursuing their personal and professional interests.

Indeed, AI offers numerous possibilities for young entrepreneurs looking to develop a profitable business. The methods presented in this book can inspire young entrepreneurs to find innovative ideas for generating passive income through AI.

However, it is important to keep in mind that implementing these methods requires skills, resources, and time. Young entrepreneurs must be realistic about income expectations and be willing to invest to succeed.

In summary, this book encourages young entrepreneurs to explore the opportunities offered by AI to generate passive income, while emphasizing the need for creativity and innovation to maximize results. The 50 methods presented are a starting point, but there are certainly many other ideas to discover and explore for ambitious entrepreneurs.